The Power Of One Leadership Playbook

By Geoffrey Ingram

Table of Contents

Acknowledgements

It takes a village to complete almost every successful endeavor, and it most certainly takes one to write a book. I want to thank everyone who has been a part of the creative process of taking this project from vision to completion.

I'd like to thank my wife and my children for their consistent support, understanding and sacrifice. I am grateful for every mentor who allowed me to glean from them.

I'd like to give credit to The Taylord Solution and Trinkat Works for their support in making sure that the Power of One Playbook came to pass the way that I envisioned it.

Finally, I am grateful to my Creator who has blessed me with the abilities, gifts, talents and skill and trusted me to help others to reach their maximum potential.

FOREWORD

Fathers in the African-American community have been misrepresented as absentee, toxic and/or poor role models. It' a powerful thing when fathers step up. It's also powerful when fathers step up and reach out reach beyond their biological family and help others in need. I am so proud to say that over the years, I have personally witnessed my friend and brother, Geoffrey Ingram be that kind of father to countless sons and daughters in the United States and Caribbean.

Geoff and I formed a friendship when I attended his Power of One Leadership Conference. We connected even further while working as colleagues on the same university campus. I have personally seen him in action, offering advice, mentoring, uplifting and being just an incredible contributor to the community at large.

This book summarizes Geoff's two decades of leadership experience, especially in the areas of marriage, fatherhood, entrepreneurship, management and ministry.

Those who have the chance to read this manuscript will be uplifted, empowered, enlightened and motivated to go forth, especially young men.

Geoff has demonstrated what leadership looks like. He is truly equipping the next generation of creative, out of the box thinkers, leaders and business professionals to start living up to their full potential.

My friend, my brother, I salute you in this great endeavor."

Dr. Rashad Richey

Dr. Rashad Richey is a Emmy nominated multi-media personality who is the Political Analyst for CBS New in Atlanta, the host of Real Talk with Rashad Richey, Chief Editor-At-Large and Sr. Writer for Rolling Out Magazine, and founder of The Rashad Richey Foundation, Inc., an organization dedicated to mentoring at-risk youth. Dr. Richey received the Presidential Lifetime Achievement Award from President Barack Obama. He is a college lecturer who has dedicated himself to being an advocate for those who need help becoming their best after a setback.

Introduction

I was a different kind of child. I always saw things differently that everyone else around me. Instead of being disappointed or amazed by the outward characteristics of an object or situation, I would automatically see the wonder in the ins, outs, design, manufacture, and purpose of something. The inner workings and big picture of life's opportunities draws me in and brings out my inner nerd.

One of the great blessings of my childhood is that my mother was an entrepreneur. She was a seamstress and an event planner/decorator. My mom was always working on a project; finishing one creation up or in the planning stages of launching another. I remember the first time that I realized that she was actually making money AND doing what she loved. I was only nine or ten years old, but finding the knowledge that people could make money, outside of a traditional job, blew my mind.

It sparked a fire in me that has never been quenched. From that moment on, I knew that I was going to be a "business person" when I grew up. What I didn't realize was that my career as a "business person" would begin long before I "grew up". In fact, it started in a very unconventional way when I was just 14 years old in the eighth grade.

It all began with three candy bars.

One day after school some of my classmates thought that they would get over on me. They asked me to sell their candy bars and bring them the proceeds. That was the deal. They didn't offer to pay me for my skill at selling the candy, or for the time that it would take me to complete the task. I was offended, until…. I got my own bright idea.

Little did my friends know, they had initiated a plan where I made a great deal more than the $3 they planned to make from selling those candy bars. You see, I suddenly remembered that I could get those candy bars a lot cheaper at the neighborhood gas station. So I accepted their offer, and used the money I made selling their candy bars to double my inventory. I sold the new inventory, paid my unwitting investors their expected $3, and purchased more inventory. By the end of the day, I had made at least $15. That is right; I made $15 by creatively turning a potentially detrimental situation around for my good.

Three candy bars started my career. There was no way that I could have planned that at all. I just identified an opportunity to make some money on my own, came up with a strategy that would help me meet my goal and executed the plan. Little did I know, the process I'd gone through that day would literally take me and my career to places I'd never thought possible or achievable.

I've used that process for the last 20 years to build and run several businesses and have an amazing career as a operations and sales leader with companies like Jiffy Lube, Five Guys Burgers and Fries, Footlocker Inc., as well as a philanthropist, mentor and minister. I've used this to train and coach thousands of teams, organizational leaders, entrepreneurs, and executives from around the world. Everything that I've put into this book is to empower you, and millions of others like you around the world, to not only dream bigger but to achieve bigger goals than you've ever thought you could.

The purpose of this leadership playbook is to cause a paradigm shift in your life. It will change the way that you think about yourself, your purpose and potential, your leadership and the way you impact the world on a daily basis. This book will challenge your perspectives of leadership, influence and your role as a leader in the world.

I didn't write this so that you could have one more inspiring book to add to your library. I created this to change your life.

I wrote it to be your personal playbook. One that you learn like the back of your hand. The playbook that you use to develop one of the most important areas of your life, your leadership skills. If used properly, the Power of One Leadership Playbook will be the secret weapon that empowers you to dominate anytime you are in a position of influence. You'll want to keep this book as a point of reference that you can read and review on a regular basis.

I wish there was a book like this when I was that fourteen year old with the heart of a mogul navigating through school, work and life. I've written the Power of One Playbook so that I can invest the best of all I've learned and experienced thus far in my career into the leaders and moguls of the future.

There are no age, race, gender or socioeconomic boundaries to who will thrive using this playbook. Leadership is a life skill that we all need and benefit from mastering. So, as you read this, take it very seriously. Take notes and engage with what you read. Answer the questions at the end of each section and chapter as thoroughly and honestly as you can. Most importantly apply what you learn immediately.

Leadership might be a brand new topic or area of focus for you. If so, I am so excited for you! You will learn some things about leadership that you wish your current and past leaders had known and applied to those positions you met them in. This will only serve to promote your growth as you move to new heights in your career.

You might already be a leader, with years of experience under your belt, and are familiar with the topics I cover. That is great! You now have a tool that you can use to better connect with and empower your team to become the leaders you need them to be!

No matter where you are in your life or career, keep this Leadership Playbook close – the same way that Popeye kept a can of spinach. You never know whose life will be impacted by you being the best leader you can be...

PART ONE

CHAPTER 1
What is The Power of One Leadership?

Over the past twenty years I've worked with, trained, coached and consulted thousands of leaders from around the world and I've noticed that you'll find average leaders and you'll find what I call Power of One Leaders. There's a huge difference between average leaders and Power of One Leaders.

Whether you find them serving in the corporate or non-profit sector, in their home, in the community or among family and friends; Power of One Leaders operate on a totally different frequency. This enables them to have a major positive impact on their environments and the teams they lead. Think about some of the most influential leaders you have worked with, heard about or admired; they are most likely Power of One Leaders.

You can easily pick the Power of One Leaders out of the crowd.

The Power of One Leadership methodology isn't something that I came up with overnight and attached it to a cool name. I created this unique and highly effective methodology while training and empowering a new team of youth leaders for my local church. At this time, I had just been ordained as a Youth Pastor and was only 27 years old. By this point in my life, I already had more than ten years of extensive leadership training and expertise from my corporate career in management and operations and through my successful entrepreneurial endeavors.

As I analyzed these experiences, I discovered that no matter what position someone worked in, they shared common traits and skills.

These characteristics are necessary for anyone to tap into their real potential. These traits would separate individuals from their peers almost instantly, whether they are in fast food, in a classroom or serving in ministry.

Since then I've had the opportunity to use this methodology in my leadership coaching and consulting business and empower hundreds of small business owners, executives, management and sales professionals, educators, administrators, ministers and students from around the globe to discover and unlock their true potential. These are the traits that I will share with you in this book and will help you to stand out and make real change in the lives of the people you serve.

Everyone Has the Ability to Become a Power of One Leader.

You have power. The definition of power is *"the ability to do something or act in a particular way, especially as a faculty or quality* or *the capacity or ability to direct or influence the behavior of others or the course of events.*

In fact, human beings are arguably the most influential and impactful species that has ever walked the face of the Earth.

In case you've never heard it, you have within yourself the innate, God-given ability and limitless potential to make an impact and influence people and your environment. Your potential is limitless and given to impact your world. This limitless power can only be limited by your beliefs and knowledge.

In order for you to tap into the Power of One Leadership that lives inside of you, you must take the limits off of what could be. Your power goes well beyond the people you meet, those you help personally or those you see benefiting from your leadership. Much of your influence and the impact you make on the world will go unseen and unrecognized by you.

As you continue to read this book, we will delve deeper into what it means to be a leader and how that translates to your personal leadership style.

Perhaps, for the first time in your life you will begin to understand how important it is to be in tune with who you are and how to unlock the infinite power to make an impact and influence the world within you!

MOMENT FOR MEDITATION

YOUR LEADERSHIP PHILOSOPHY

Take some time to think about the ideas that are below.

IDEA 1: "One Person can change the world." Rosa Parks

IDEA 2: "One person cannot change the world; yet the world can change because of one person." Ronald Janovsky

In the space provided, explain which one most aligns with your current philosophy of leadership and why? Think about what it means to be a leader and how you fit into your definition of leadership.

Your Thoughts

_____

_____

_____

_____

_____

_____

_____

_____

_____

_____

MOMENT FOR MEDITATION

YOUR LEADERSHIP PHILOSOPHY

_____

_____

_____

_____

_____

_____

_____

_____

_____

_____

_____

_____

_____

_____

_____

_____

_____

_____

Chapter 2
Leadership 101"

As this is the *Playbook for Leaders*, it is imperative that you know exactly what I mean every time you see the word "leadership" mentioned in this book.

LEAD

The word lead has a very interesting history. Linguists have not found a word that translates to our current understanding of the word leader that occurs before 900. The word "lead" comes from the Old English word *lædan* , which means a variety of things:

- to cause to go with oneself
- march at the front of
- go before as a guide
- accompany and show the way
- carry on
- sprout forth
- bring forth
- pass (one's life)
- go, travel); cognate with Dutch*leiden,* German *leiten,* Old Norse *leitha*

Today "lead" means to guide, impact and influence.

ER

"Er" is a suffix that adds to the meaning of its root word. Er means someone who does

SHIP

Adding the second suffix "ship" means the art or craft of doing something.

LEAD + ER + SHIP = the way that a person uses their influence.

The etymology of the word "lead" digs deep into the reality and role of a leader. Most people don't realize that leadership begins well before you receive the call or request to serve. Your leadership begins from the moment of conception. Once you came into existence, you immediately began to influence impact and transform your mother physically, mentally and emotionally.

Consider that one of the first meanings of the Old English word *lædan* deals with an action that motivates others to move. In this chapter, we will be discussing the different types and levels of leaders so that you can assess yourself and create a growth plan. True leaders understand that in order to lead others, they must lead their own lives with courage, humility and wisdom. As you are going through this playbook, consider how you are using your influence to affect change in your business, corporation, ministry, family and relationships.

MOMENT FOR MEDITATION

LEADERSHIP

Write your personal definition of a leader.

_____

_____

_____

_____

_____

_____

_____

_____

_____

_____

_____

_____

_____

_____

_____

_____

_____

_____

Do you fit into what you described above? Please explain.

_____

_____

_____

_____

_____

_____

_____

_____

_____

_____

_____

_____

_____

_____

_____

_____

_____

_____

_____

LEADERSHIP

List 3 leaders who have made an impact on your life and if their impact was negative or positive. Give your reasons for each choice.
(You don't have to give their names. Their position is fine)
Leader #1

_____

_____

_____

_____

_____

_____

Leader #2

_____

_____

_____

_____

_____

_____

Leader #3

_____

_____

_____

_____

_____

_____

TYPES OF LEADERSHIP

There are two types of leaders: *passive leaders* and *active/intentional leaders*.

THE PASSIVE LEADER

A **passive leader** is someone who has the authority, influence and ability to cause change, but chooses to maintain an inactive role. The most common type of leader today is the passive one. The world is full of organizations that have passive leaders in their ranks.

Why would someone with the ability to affect change and make things better choose to remain silent and frozen? Well there are many reasons, but the most common reasons usually stem from the way that these cocooned leaders were taught as children.

When we are not encouraged to express our beliefs and opinions or speak up for ourselves as children, we often fall into the trap of silence.

This is a dangerous place for many because, without intervention, they will remain frozen in place wishing that they could only do something different.

Oftentimes, passive leaders don't even recognize that they have been imprisoned because inaction has become a way of life for them.

When a passive leader becomes free, they also unlock the greatness and change that has been waiting in the people who hold them in high esteem.

THE ACTIVE/INTENTIONAL LEADER

The **active/intentional leader**; however, is characterized by taking action rather than thinking without movement. An active leader moves when the need arises. This ability and desire to take massive and or immediate action is what causes these leaders to be extraordinary and influence others to change.

This type of leader is actively engaged in the direction their life is headed personally, professionally and within their community. When you are an active leader, you address personal issues, tend to your relationships and keep your eyes focused on maintaining a healthy balance. Reaching personal goals and influencing others is a priority.

An active, engaged leader is often instrumental in helping a passive leader break out into leadership. The *Leadership Playbook* has been designed to teach you how to be the most effective in the way that you influence those you have been assigned to help reach their goals.

Intentional leaders have purpose led interactions that serve to further their reach and progress. This type of leader leaves nothing up to chance and knows that a great plan requires research, careful analysis, execution and consistent action.

Power of One Leaders are active and intentional, taking the necessary steps to get their team members to the goal line. Super leaders know that their members may not be at the same level and are prepared to put in the work to bring everyone to the table with the needed contributions to get the job done well. As you move through the Play Book, you're going to find out how you can operate as a Super Leader and influence others to become their best. It's time to dig deep to find out where you are.

MOMENT FOR MEDITATION

LEADERSHIP TYPES

Are you or have you ever been a passive leader? Please explain your

answer.

_____

_____

_____

_____

_____

_____

_____

_____

_____

_____

If you answered yes, what were the circumstances surrounding you becoming passive? If you answered no, what caused you to take charge of how you lead?

_____

_____

_____

_____

_____

_____

_____

_____

MOMENT FOR MEDITATION

LEADERSHIP TYPES

Are you or have you ever been an active/intentional leader? If yes, what pieces of advice would you give to other active leaders or to passive leaders who are ready to impact their team more effectively?

_____

_____

_____

_____

_____

_____

_____

_____

_____

_____

_____

LEVELS OF LEADERSHIP

There are 3 levels of leadership: Aspiring, Emerging, Established

ASPIRING LEADERS

Aspiring Leaders know what they want to do, who they want to lead and where they want to go; but they are still looking for opportunities to get as much experience and training in their field of work. Leaders at this level are still "unproven" in the eyes of general society; and find it difficult to invest in their own growth because their network, experience and/or resources may be very limited.

EMERGING LEADERS

Emerging Leaders have been successful and consistent seizing as every opportunity to network, gain experience, cultivate their craft and actively work in their area of specialty. These leaders are the ones who are constantly on the move and looking for innovative ways to initiate change and establish their reputation. Emerging leaders need to be careful of burnout and take time to re-group and dig deeply into personal development so that they are able to handle the stressors that come with active leadership.

Emerging leaders are often peer leaders. They are usually the supervisors or group leaders within the organization. Their activities as managers allow them to master this level and become established.

ESTABLISHED LEADERS

Established Leaders are experienced and seasoned in their field, or area of service, and have grown to the point where their organization is creating opportunities for others to become leaders. They openly share the knowledge and wisdom they obtained from years of experience and training. Established leaders have solid financial backing and know how to wisely invest and save their resources.

Leadership does not only happen in the marketplace or in organizations. If you have answered the need in any environment to help move people from one destination to another, you were their leader.

22

MOMENT FOR MEDITATION

LEADERSHIP LEVELS

Are you an Aspiring, Emerging or Established Leader? Please explain how you came to your answer and how you plan to ascend to the next level of leadership.

_____

_____

_____

_____

_____

_____

_____

_____

_____

_____

_____

PART TWO
READY FOR ACTION

Intention, personal development and planning go hand in hand for the successful leader. If you want to be a healthy and effective leader, make time to develop creative strategies and growth opportunities for yourself and your team.

Your plan of action starts with your identification of 3 things:

1. Your identity

2. Your vision

3. Your resources

The process of identification requires more than simple observation. True identification necessitates that you analyze the information that you receive so that when it is time to take action, you can make informed choices.

You need to know who you are, where you are going, and what is in your toolbox that will enable you to make your maximum level of impact.

In the following chapters, you will receive instructions on how to properly identify those three crucial areas and develop a winning game plan. Any good coach, or talented athlete will tell you that natural ability without planning or training can only get you so far.

So let's get into it and start planning your growth journey.

Chapter 3
Your Identity: Who Are You?

Leaders are people too! Whether you are using this playbook for your own personal development or as a training tool for your leadership staff, you must never forget one truth.

"Good Leaders Can Motivate Others to Action. Great Leaders Know How to Initiate Personal Change."

As you are moving through the Playbook, remember that it is crucial that you take the time necessary to find out who you are, what makes you tick and what sets you apart from your cohorts. In short, you need to be clear about *your* identity.

Your identity is a tangible thing. It is "the state of having unique characteristics held by no other person or thing."[1] You are unique and even though your personality type or leadership style may be similar to others, you should never attempt to be a carbon copy of anyone else.

There is so much more to you than your personality, gifts and character traits.

Your personal identity is also determined by:

- Your family background
    - ✓ Childhood experiences
    - ✓ Financial experiences
    - ✓ Relational experiences

- Your spiritual beliefs
    - ✓ Do you believe in a Higher Intelligent Power?

- ✓ Are you an Atheist or Agnostic?
- ✓ Spiritual Experiences

- How you interact with the world
  - ✓ Your reactions to people and events

- How you make decisions
  - ✓ Is your decision making process based on outside or internal sources?

- How you organize your time
  - ✓ Do you control your time or does it control you?

Being honest with yourself about your identity is crucial and is not always the easiest thing to do. The journey to knowing your true self will not be complete by the end of this book, but you will have a good idea of the inner workings of your mind, soul and emotions. These are key areas that influence your worldview and how others receive from you.

You form your Self-Identity with each new encounter, relationship and experience. In the following Moment for Meditation, you are going to tell us how you currently self-identify.

Doing this before you go through any of the Playbook exercises will give you an opportunity to become aware of any areas of your identity that need to be explored, developed or strengthened..

MOMENT FOR MEDITATION

SELF-IDENTIFICATION

Who are you? Describe yourself as honestly as you can.

Do not look anything up. Do not ask others for their perceptions. Be honest and write down the person you see when you look in the mirror every morning.

_____

_____

_____

_____

_____

_____

_____

_____

_____

_____

_____

_____

_____

_____

_____

_____

_____

_____

_____

_____

_____

_____

_____

_____

_____

Now that your juices are flowing and you are thinking about what makes you tick, it is time to explore your temperament, or the moral fiber of what makes you unique.

Your temperament is the foundation of who you are and is the part of your personality that you inherited. There are certain behavioral tendencies and instincts that are set on automatic. These instincts and behaviors are genetic so they can be extremely difficult to change, but nothing is impossible.

Knowing where you land in the four basic temperaments will help you to understand your strengths and weaknesses, while equipping you to handle interpersonal relationships effectively and with care.

The Four Basic Temperaments

CHOLERIC | THE LION | ANALYST

The Lion is rational, analytical and extremely passionate. As an extrovert, it seems that the lion is a natural born leader whose ambition, organizational skills, strong will and quick actions make it easy for others to trust and follow the vision.

SANGUINE| THE OTTER | ARTISAN

The Otter, also known as the "talker" is an impulsive, energetic, intelligent, pleasure-seeking extrovert whose keen perception is second to none. The Otter is all about innovation and is not afraid to take risks to cross the finish line with pizazz and excitement. Their ability to relate well to others allows the otter to build key relationships with those who will take care of the details so that they can get to their BIG IDEA.

MELANCHOLY | BEAVER | GUARDIAN

The Beaver is the introverted thinker of the group. The beaver has very high standards for themselves and those who surround them. These standards drive how they interact with others and solve problems. Beavers are creatively analytical and have great organizational skills. These guardians have no problem upholding their standards through accountability and assistance.

PHLEGMATIC | DIPLOMAT | GOLDEN RETRIEVER

The Golden Retriever is the introverted watcher who is relaxed, sympathetic and very sociable. Golden Retrievers are idealists who bases their actions on principles rather than excitement, logic or practicality. These types of leaders often gain followers based on their passion for doing the right thing and their commitment to results.

MOMENT FOR MEDITATION

Do you believe you are naturally a Lion, Golden Retriever, Beaver or Otter? Do you feel like you are a mixture of some of these temperaments?

How did you come to that conclusion?

_____

_____

_____

_____

_____

_____

_____

_____

_____

_____

Keep these descriptions in mind as you continue this chapter so that you can begin to locate yourself. Even though you did not choose your temperament, you do have the opportunity to make improvements.

These changes will require consistency and persistence to achieve the results that you desire; but you can make them happen. Then you will need to set up boundaries that battle against your natural tendencies towards any unproductive or defeating behaviors.

Your temperament is the canvas underlying who you are and your personality is the painting on the canvas. Your personality is what happens when you add your learned habits, perception and behavior to your temperament.

According to Walter Mishel, personality is "the typical behavioral patterns (including emotions and thoughts) that characterize a person's adaptation to the events of life."

In short, your personality is how you identify with the world. The way that you are wired determines how you filter the 60,000 thoughts or bits of information that come across your brain every day. There is not one way to define personality, because we all have unique experiences and perceptions that determine who we have become.

At the end of this chapter, you will find a simple personality quiz to help you to get a better idea of how you interact with the world around you and how you make decisions.

Master Your Mind

The human mind is an amazing organ. There are two areas of our minds: the conscious level and the subconscious level.

The thoughts that you think purposely happen on the conscious level. Your subconscious mind is created by what you habitually think about and experience.

"Your subconscious mind is the seat of your emotions and is the creative mind."[2] Emotions come naturally from the brain and are crucial to how your brain directs information from the subconscious to the conscious mind.

The subconscious mind is the most powerful part of your mind; however, you can consciously influence it through disciplined and focused effort.

The conscious mind is what you actively do, so if you are actively moving towards what you deem to be important, this will greatly influence your subconscious mind.

Many schools of thought refer to our ability to affect the way that our mind works. Christian dogma is very clear that we are to work out our own soul's salvation or figure out what triggers us to produce good fruit and what causes us to move outside of the realm of acceptable behavior. A number of religions teach their practitioners that success depends on their level of belief.

Simply put, you can do anything that you set your mind and heart to do because your belief fuels your intensity and follow through. This statement is one of the truest descriptions of human identity, yet so many of us don't realize that we can ultimately determine our success, even if we can't control how we get there.

MOMENT FOR MEDITATION

DO YOU BELIEVE?

"You can do anything that you set your mind and heart to do." Do you agree or disagree with this statement? What have you experienced that gives you the foundation for your explanation?

_____

_____

_____

_____

_____

_____

_____

_____

_____

_____

The Will to Do More

Most people live their lives mimicking someone else's impact on the world. That is not the way that you were created to live.

It is up to you to choose to become who you were meant to be. I will refer to this choice as your will. Your will, or choices, play a huge part in the direction of your life. Your expressed desire to do anything is your will.

The power to choose is a gift that comes with great responsibility. What will you do with this great gift?

Will you become a developing leader who shows others how to become their best self, or will you try to fit into a mold that was created for someone else?

The choice is yours.

MOMENT FOR MEDITATION

POWER OF CHOICE

Did you know that you have agency, or power to enact change, in your life? Why or why not?

_____

_____

_____

_____

_____

MOMENT FOR MEDITATION

POWER OF CHOICE

What will you do with your power to choose? Think of all of the situations that require intervention in your life, career, business, ministry or team. What can you do to enact change?

_____

_____

_____

_____

_____

_____

_____

_____

_____

Do you feel like you have enough information to make the proper choices for your future? What questions do you think need to be answered?

_____

_____

_____

_____

_____

_____

_____

_____

_____

YOUR IDENTITY:

ALL IN THE FAMILY

Your family background and upbringing play a huge part in who you have become today.

You see the world through the filters that developed as you experienced life through the innocent and immature eyes of childhood.

Take the time to dig into the foundation that caused you to flourish or given you the drive to never quit. Allow yourself permission to search through your memories to see why you always want to help others, or why you feel like you have to be in control.

This is a safe place for you to be honest and raw without judgement.

Be willing to forgive wrongdoings, and determined to forgive yourself, no matter what.

MOMENT FOR MEDITATION

YOUR IDENTITY

Were your parents happily married? If not, did they co-parent well?

_____

_____

_____

_____

_____

Did your parent's relationship with each other affect what you
thought about yourself? (If so, how?)

_____

_____

_____

_____

_____

YOUR IDENTITY

How were your childhood relationships with your siblings? How are those relationships today? Are they better or worse? Explain.

_____

_____

_____

_____

_____

_____

_____

_____

_____

Did you grow up in a financially comfortable environment or did your family experience difficulties regularly? How does this affect the way that you deal with your personal or organization's finances today?

_____

_____

_____

_____

_____

_____

_____

_____

_____

_____

_____

_____

YOUR IDENTITY:

HOW YOU SEE THE WORLD

You are a spiritual being. Even if you believe that there is no God, it would be difficult to deny that we are more than just flesh and blood. All of us are spiritual beings having a physical experience here on the earth. As a spirit, it is essential that you are clear about the reasons that you believe the way you do and assess them from an intellectual point of view.

Your worldview is an important component to how you interact with your environment and those around you. Moreover, your worldview can actually determine if you are successful because it is what drives your actions and the motives of your heart.

Let's get into it.

MOMENT FOR MEDITATION

SPIRITUAL BACKGROUND

Do you believe in an Intelligent Higher Power?
___Yes (Go to ITEM 2)

___No (Go to ITEM 3)

___Unsure (Go to ITEM 4)

ITEM 2
Why do you believe in a Higher Power?

_____

_____

_____

_____

_____

_____

_____

SPIRITUAL BACKGROUND

ITEM 2 continued

Have your spiritual experiences fueled your belief or did you inherit it through tradition? Explain.

_____

_____

_____

_____

_____

_____

_____

_____

_____

_____

Do you belong to an organized religion?

_____

_____

_____

What are the tenets of your faith?

_____

_____

_____

_____

_____

_____

MOMENT FOR MEDITATION

SPIRITUAL BACKGROUND

ITEM 2

Do your spiritual beliefs influence the way that you make decisions and interact with others?

_____

_____

_____

_____

_____

_____

_____

_____

_____

Does your belief system affect the way that you see your place in the world?

_____

_____

_____

_____

_____

_____

Please describe your moral system.

_____

_____

_____

_____

_____

_____

ITEM 3

Why do believe there is no Higher Power?

_____

_____

_____

_____

_____

_____

Have you ever believed in a Higher Power? If yes, please write a brief explanation of what caused you to change your mind.

_____

_____

_____

_____

_____

_____

_____

SPIRITUAL BACKGROUND

ITEM 3 (Continued)

Have your spiritual experiences (or lack thereof) fueled your belief or did you inherit it through tradition?

_____

_____

_____

_____

Please describe your moral system.

_____

_____

_____

_____

_____

_____

What do you believe is your place in this world?

_____

_____

_____

_____

_____

_____

MOMENT FOR MEDITATION

SPIRITUAL BACKGROUND

ITEM 4

What are your spiritual beliefs?

_____

_____

_____

_____

_____

_____

What spiritual matters are important to you?

_____

_____

_____

_____

_____

_____

SPIRITUAL BACKGROUND

ITEM 4(Continued)
Please describe your moral system.

_____

_____

_____

_____

_____

_____

What do you believe is your place in this world?

_____

_____

_____

_____

_____

_____

The next section of this chapter is the short personality quiz. The quiz will give you a more specific view of who you are and how you identify with the world.

PERSONALITY QUIZ

In order to get the most accurate results, answer each question as honestly as possible. Don't worry about what others will think of your responses. Be comfortable with who you are so that you can make the most impact in your world.

Instructions: Check the response to the question that best describes you.

1. How do you prefer to spend your free time?

____ Home Alone (I)

___ Out with others (E)

2. Fill in the blank: I _____ social gatherings and meeting new people.

___ Avoid (I)

___ Enjoy (E)

3. How would you describe yourself?

___ Private and reserved (I)

___ Social and outgoing (E)

4. Would you prefer to focus on _____?

___ Facts, details and steps (S)

___ Concepts, theories and the bigger picture (IN)

5. Which do you tend to appreciate?

___ What can only be imagined (IN)

___ Practical and proven things (S)

6. Do you prefer to be _____?

___ Realistic, relying on common sense (S)

___ Imaginative, doing it your own way (IN)

7. How do you tend to make decisions?

___ With your heart, feelings and emotions (F)

___ With your head using reasoning and logic (T)

8. How do you prefer to engage with others?

___ Up close and personal (F)

___ Somewhat distant and objectively (T)

9. Which one of the following have you been accused of most often?

___ Being too emotional (F)

___ Being too cold (T)

10. Complete this statement: I view structure and organization as _____.

___ Restricting (P)

___ Liberating (J)

11. Complete this statement: I prefer activities to be _____.

___ Structured and planned out (J)

___ Unstructured and spontaneous (P)

12. Complete this statement: I prefer to _____.

___ Control my environment (J)

___ Go with the flow (P)

PERSONALITY QUIZ RESULTS

Go back and look over your answers. There are letters after each answer. Tally up the total of each letter and see where you fit in.

YOUR RESULTS

TOTAL	TYPES
____	❖ I = Introvert
____	❖ E = Extrovert
____	❖ S = Sensing
____	❖ IN = Intuitive
____	❖ T = Thinking
____	❖ F = Feeling
____	❖ J = Judging
____	❖ P = Perceiving

A Breakdown of Personality Combinations[3]

Use these results to help you understand your strengths, weaknesses and the best way for you to initiate change through problem solving and brainstorming.

(The following descriptions were taken completely from "The 16 Personality Types in a Nutshell" by Jaroslaw Jankowski)

The Administrator (ESTJ)	The Advocate (ESFJ):
Administrators are hard working, responsible and extremely loyal. Energetic and decisive, they value order, stability, security and clear rules. They are matter-of-fact and businesslike, logical, rational and practical and possess the capability to assimilate large amounts of detailed information.	Advocates are well organized, energetic and enthusiastic. Practical, responsible and conscientious, they are sincere and exceptionally gregarious. Advocates are perceptive of human feelings, emotions and needs and take great delight in helping other people solve their problems.
The Animator (ESTP)	**The Practitioner (ISTP)**
Animators are energetic, active and enterprising. They are fond of the company of others and are inspirers and instigators of action. These pragmatic realists find abstract solutions hard to swallow and prefer concrete action plans.	Practitioners are optimistic and spontaneous, with a positive approach to life. Reserved and independent, they hold true to their personal convictions and view external principles with skepticism. They will trade abstract concepts and solutions for a productive time of hard work with tangible results.
The Counsellor (ENFJ)	**The Director (ENTJ)**
Counsellors are optimistic, enthusiastic and quick-witted. They are courteous and tactful with an extraordinary gift for empathy. Counsellors find joy in selflessly helping others. They are skilled in finding other people's hidden potential and giving them the faith to believe in themselves and take action.	Directors are independent, active and decisive. Rational, logical and creative, when they analyze problems, they look at the bigger picture, foresee future consequences and can create concrete plans of action from theoretical concepts. Directors are generally optimistic and have a healthy sense of their worth.

The Enthusiast (ENFP)	The Logician (INTP)
Enthusiasts are energetic, enthusiastic and optimistic. Capable of enjoying life and looking ahead to the future, they are dynamic, quick-witted and creative. The Enthusiast is a "people person" and value honest, genuine relationships. These empathetic individuals infect others with their enthusiasm and are often at the center of events.	Logicians are original, resourceful and creative. With a love for solving theoretical problems, they are analytical, quick-witted, and enthusiastically disposed towards new concepts. Logicians have the innate ability to connect individual events to create rules and theories from them. They are quick to spot confusion and inconsistency because of their logical and inquisitive nature.

A Breakdown of Personality Combinations[4]

(The following descriptions were taken completely from "The 16 Personality Types in a Nutshell" by Jaroslaw Jankowski)

The Mentor (INFJ)	The Presenter (ESFP)
Mentors are creative and sensitive. With their gaze firmly fixed on the future, they spot opportunities and potential that are imperceptible to others. These individuals are idealists and visionaries who are geared towards helping people.	Presenters are optimistic, energetic and outgoing with the ability to enjoy life and have fun to the full. They love being at the center of attention and are practical, flexible and spontaneous with the ability to arouse the interest and enthusiasm of their listeners.
The Protector (ISFJ)	**The Strategist (INTJ)**
Protectors are sincere, warm-hearted, unassuming, trustworthy and extraordinarily loyal. With their ability to perceive people's needs and their desire to help them, they will always put others first. Practical, well organized and gifted with both an eye and a memory for detailed, they are responsible, hardworking, patient, persevering and capable of seeing things through to the end.	Strategists are independent and outstandingly individualists, with an immense stream of inner energy. Creative, inventive and resourceful, others perceive them as competent, self-assured and distant. Strategist always look at the bigger picture and have a driving urge to improve the world around them and set it in order.

The Counsellor (ENFJ)	The Director (ENTJ)
Counsellors are optimistic, enthusiastic and quick-witted. They are courteous and tactful with an extraordinary gift for empathy. Counsellors find joy in selflessly helping others. They are skilled in finding other people's hidden potential and giving them the faith to believe in themselves and take action.	Directors are independent, active and decisive. Rational, logical and creative, when they analyze problems, they look at the bigger picture, foresee future consequences and can create concrete plans of action from theoretical concepts. Directors are generally optimistic and have a healthy sense of their worth.
The Innovator (ENTP)	**The Inspector (ISTJ)**
Innovators are inventive, original and independent. Optimistic, energetic and enterprising, they are people of action who love being at the center of events and solving insoluble problems. The Innovator often thinks about the future and is a natural visionary who is open to new concepts and ideas.	Inspectors are people who can always be counted on. Well-mannered, punctual, reliable, conscientious and responsible, when they give their word, they keep it. Inspectors can be seen as serious, cold and reserved because of their analytical, methodical and systematic nature. They value stability, calm environments and consistency.
The Artist (ISFP)	**The Idealist (INFP)**
Artists are sensitive, creative and original, with a sense of the aesthetic and natural artistic talents. These independent individuals follow their own value system, are very optimistic and love living in the moment	Idealists are sensitive, loyal and creative. It is extremely important to an idealist to live according to their values. They are very interested in spiritual matters and delve deeply into the mysteries of life

MOMENT FOR MEDITATION

Your personality

You should have a good idea of who you are, who you want to be, your spiritual beliefs and how you interact with the world. Take some time to synthesize this information to get a coherent picture of your leadership and personality style.

Which temperament do you identify with most closely (Lion, Otter, Golden Retriever, Beaver)? Explain your choice.

_____

_____

_____

_____

_____

_____

_____

_____

_____

_____

_____

Which personality type(s) describe you? Explain your choice(s). You may find yourself in more than one of these descriptions, so dig deep and explain the similarities and differences that you find most striking.

_____

_____

_____

_____

_____

_____

_____

_____

_____

_____

_____

_____

MOMENT FOR MEDITATION

Your personality

As you look at your temperament and personality category, and relate it to your experiences, where do you thrive and where is there room for your improvement?

List Your Strengths:

_____

_____

_____

_____

_____

_____

List Your Areas for Development

_____

_____

_____

_____

_____

_____

Chapter 4
The Vision

If you have ever researched how to start a business, run a company, create a non-profit organization, lead your family, or lay out your life-plan, there is one word that is ALWAYS present.

That word is vision.

Now the dictionary says that vision is the act or power of seeing.

Vision is also defined as a thought, concept or object formed by the imagination.

When someone asks you for your vision, what should you say? Should you communicate what you see currently or what you have imagined?

Let's get into it.

VISION CASTING

When you hear the word vision, what comes to mind? Do you believe that communicating your vision means articulating what you currently see in your organization; OR does it mean detailing what you imagine? How did you come to this conclusion?

_____

_____

_____

_____

_____

_____

"The Best Vision is Insight." Malcom Forbes

Your vision for an organization, group, business or movement perceives your current reality, while spelling out what could be.

In order to have a vision, you must first be able to see physically and spiritually. You must be able to identify characteristics, processes, procedures, profits, losses, failures and successes with your natural senses; and perceive the underlying factors behind what works well and what needs to be improved.

When you are casting the vision for the future of your organization by detailing the possibilities that you see on the canvas of your imagination, you are using your spiritual eye. You need both the ability to see the present and to imagine how different the future can look in order to cast a successful, engaging vision.

"Leadership is about vision and ability, not power." Seth Berkley

What do you think is the most important trait for leaders to use when vision casting?

_____

_____

_____

_____

_____

_____

CASTING THE VISION

If you have ever been to a presentation where the speaker uses a projector to show pictures on a screen, then you have been the recipient of vision casting.

Vision casting is more than just talking about your hopes and dreams for the future of the organization, business or movement. It is the word picture that you paint on canvas of the imaginations of your members that points them into the direction of what the future will look like for your business.

Having a vision that is unique and inspiring is very powerful. It has the ability to move people to unified action to arrive at a common destination. When humans join for one purpose, they are almost unstoppable. Your vision has the power to rally the efforts, talents and skills of your members and partners in support of your goals.

While you are leading others, you also need to have a plan in place to lead your own life.

Your personal vision details how you see the best version of yourself. That includes your training, experiences, emotional intelligence, relationships, spiritual well being, etc.

MOMENT FOR MEDITATION

YOUR PERSONAL VISION

Please write your personal vision. If you have never written it

_____

_____

_____

_____

_____

_____

_____

_____

_____

_____

YOUR CAREER VISION

Write the vision that you have for your career. Are you an entrepreneur or will you advance to a certain position within your industry to exact change? Do you desire a career change? etc

_____

_____

_____

_____

_____

_____

_____

_____

_____

_____

YOUR FAMILY VISION

What is your vision of family? Describe "your" ideal family and the role that you play or will play in its success.

_____

_____

_____

_____

_____

_____

_____

_____

_____

_____

_____

How did you come up with your vision statement? Did you base it on the thoughts and opinions of others or on your desire for certain outcomes?

When you have the privilege of setting the path for your organization, department, company, or association, it is important that you begin with the correct mindset. Your mind should be set on fulfilling the values of what you have been assigned to represent, not on the approval or acceptance of others.

Your Vision Must Be Unique

The vision that your organization has should be your own. Even if your business or ministry exists in partnership with another movement, you must be careful to keep your goals specific to your specialty. Having a unique vision does not mean that you are going to try to re-invent the wheel. That is unwise. It just means that the future that you want your members to work to create is what you see in your mind's eye and not something that another person dreamt up.

You Are Going to Need Faith

Faith is confidence or trust in a person or thing. First, you are going to need to believe that your vision is possible. You see, casting a vision is more than just creating fantasy stories of what could be. Your vision is what <u>will be</u> when it is accompanied with corresponding action.

Actually, if you can imagine it, then you can believe it. Our brains are funny that way. When it creates an idea or picture, it processes that idea as a reality. That is how faith and confidence works together to give you the ability to accomplish things that seem impossible.

Your confidence in the probability of reaching the goal is of the utmost importance. Your belief in the idea of what you see will fuel your passion and your progress. It will push you to seek help when you need it, and to let go of the false premise that you are a one-person show. Your vision is much bigger than you. It should be about creating a profound change that impacts the world around you and causes others to meet their own goals.

MOMENT FOR MEDITATION

VISION CASTING

Are the vision statements that you just wrote BIG? Are they bigger
than you and what you can see with your natural eye? If not, explore
the reason behind this and expand. If your answer is yes, who will
be impacted once your vision is fulfilled?

_____

_____

_____

_____

_____

_____

_____

_____

_____

_____

Begin With The End in Mind

If you do not know your destination, how will you create the map? It is near impossible to set a course to get somewhere specific when you do not know where that place is. In order to know what your organization will look like once you have accomplished the mission, you need to know the mission. The mission statement gives the purpose and drive behind the vision.

GET CLEAR ON YOUR MISSION

As we move to one of the most important parts of creating your winning plays, it is time to turn your thoughts towards your organization, ministry or team.

What is your mission statement?

_____

_____

_____

_____

_____

_____

_____

_____

_____

What are the goals and targets that your organization are looking to hit?

_____

_____

_____

_____

_____

_____

_____

_____

_____

MOMENT FOR MEDITATION

GET CLEAR ON YOUR MISSION

Who do you serve?

_____

_____

_____

_____

_____

_____

_____

_____

_____

What is your why?

_____

_____

_____

_____

_____

_____

_____

_____

_____

MOMENT FOR MEDITATION

VISION BUILDING

Write your current vision statement:

_____

_____

_____

_____

_____

_____

_____

_____

_____

_____

_____

_____

Does your vision line up with the mission statement that you previously wrote? Explain.

_____

_____

_____

_____

_____

_____

_____

_____

_____

_____

_____

_____

_____

MOMENT FOR MEDITATION

VISION BUILDING

What is the focus of your role within the organization?

_____

_____

_____

_____

_____

What do your constituents and/or superiors want to see in the

_____

_____

_____

_____

_____

What are your goals as it relates to what your shareholders want to see?

_____

_____

_____

_____

_____

_____

_____

_____

_____

_____

_____

_____

VISION BUILDING

Take as long as you need for this next question. Research. Look at other successful leaders. Get clear with your intentions.

Remember your mission and write the vision or what it will look like when your organization or team reaches its goals.

_____

_____

_____

_____

_____

_____

_____

_____

_____

_____

_____

EVALUATE THE VISION

Is your current vision bigger than you are? Others should be able to pick up the baton and carry out the vision that you've cast.

_____

_____

_____

_____

_____

_____

_____

_____

_____

_____

_____

_____

Do you have faith that is possible? Do you believe that you can do what you've seen on the canvas of your imagination?

_____

_____

_____

_____

_____

_____

_____

_____

_____

_____

_____

_____

EVALUATE THE VISION

Does your vision show others what your organization would look like once you've accomplished your mission or does it add more to the mission statement?

_____

_____

_____

_____

_____

_____

_____

_____

_____

_____

_____

Chapter 5

Strategize

Now that you know where the goal is located, it is time to create a winning strategy so that you are prepared to navigate your way to victory. A strategy is a plan, method or series of maneuvers for obtaining a specific goal or result.[5] Your strategy will determine how you plan your action steps.

I designed The Power of One Leadership Playbook to show you how to create a diagram for each of the members of your team to follow while they are working make a touchdown and manifest your vision.

Winning plays (strategies) are the result of research, wisdom, and careful planning. Knowing where you are going is just part of the battle.

You will need to put in some time assessing your different options and opportunities and determining what could delay your progress so that you can make the necessary preparations.

Do Your Homework

Find Your Fan Base

Your fans are the people who will partake from what you offer, as well as your supporters. Who will partake in the product/service that your business, non-profit, social club, church offers? Write a profile of your perfect fan. Include the gender, income, marital status, geographic location, interests, hobbies, occupation, and family dynamic.

MOMENT FOR MEDITATION

Your fan base

What Sex is Your Ideal Fan? Why?

_____

_____

_____

What is the age range? Why?

_____

_____

_____

What is their income? What is their disposable income? Why?

_____

_____

_____

Are they married, divorced, single, or does it matter? Why or why not?

_____

_____

Where are they located geographically? (City or small town? Is there a specific area? Are they internationally based?) Why does this matter?

_____

_____

_____

_____

_____

_____

Your Fan Base

What are their interests? (Where will you find them in their free time?)

_____

_____

_____

_____

_____

_____

What is their religious preference? Does it matter?

_____

_____

_____

_____

_____

Now it's time to put all of this data into one description that will give you an idea of who you are serving.

MOMENT FOR MEDITATION

Your Fan Profile

Write out a cohesive description of who they are so that you know how to communicate with them, find them, and meet their needs as your organization progresses.

_____

_____

_____

_____

_____

_____

_____

_____

_____

_____

_____

_____

MOMENT FOR MEDITATION

WHAT'S THE PLAY?

It's time to figure out how you are going to get to your end goal. I'm here to tell you that you do not have to re-invent the wheel to do great things. Use the gift of other people's experience to help you succeed.

Look at different organizations that are currently displaying your vision and research them. How did they accomplish their goals? How long did it take? Look at what they have done well and what areas that they need to improve.

List some organizations with mission statements and visions that are similar to that of your organization.

_____   _____

_____   _____

_____   _____

Find organizations that have been successful in fulfilling their mission statement (these organizations do not have to be within your field).

_____   _____

_____   _____

_____   _____

MOMENT FOR MEDITATION

COMPETITION RESEARCH

Organization #1:_____

Mission Statement/Vision:

_____

_____

_____

_____

_____

What have they done well?

_____

_____

_____

_____

_____

What would you do differently? What could they have improved to reach the goal more effectively?

_____

_____

_____

_____

_____

COMPETITION RESEARCH

Organization 2:_____

Mission Statement/Vision:

_____

_____

_____

_____

_____

What have they done well?

_____

_____

_____

_____

_____

What would you do differently? What could they have improved to reach the goal more effectively?

_____

_____

_____

_____

_____

MOMENT FOR MEDITATION

COMPETITION RESEARCH

Organization #3:_____ _____

Mission Statement/Vision:

_____

_____

_____

_____

_____

What have they done well?

_____

_____

_____

_____

_____

What would you do differently? What could they have improved to reach the goal more effectively?

_____

_____

_____

_____

_____

COMPETITORS

Non-profits, social organizations, churches, or commercial businesses all have competition that vying for the attention, money and time of its members, customers and potential supporters.

List some of your competitors and their offers.

Competitor #1:

_____

Their Offer:

_____

_____

_____

Competitor #2:

_____

Their Offer:

_____

_____

_____

_____

Competitor #3:

_____

Their Offer:

_____

_____

_____

MOMENT FOR MEDITATION

COMPETITORS

What strategies will you use to keep the attention and support of your audience?

_____

_____

_____

_____

_____

BRAINSTORMING SPACE

_____

_____

_____

_____

_____

_____

BRAINSTORMING SPACE

YOU NEED A COACH

Now that you have done your homework, it's time to build your team and find the right coach. A good coach will help you to look at the big picture and think outside of the box. This person should be someone who has reached the level of success that you are looking to attain and be able to invest in your progress.

Who are the most influential people in your life right now?

_____   _____

_____   _____

_____   _____

Who is available and willing to assist you in your endeavors?

_____   _____

_____   _____

_____   _____

Reach out to your coach during your tenure to get out of the box advice and wisdom on how to proceed when you need direction.

Build Your Team

Find a team of people who are invested in the success of your vision. These team members must have the capacity to learn, work together, think creatively and independently, and be self-starters.

You'll need someone who is able to rally the group in your absence, analytical thinkers, creative minds, scribes, rule followers and rule breakers.

Make sure that you look at the personality profiles earlier in the book as you interview and/or select your team.

MOMENT FOR MEDITATION

WHO IS ON YOUR TEAM?

What roles will you need on your planning & execution team to succeed?

Role 1:

_____

Role Description:_____

_____

_____

_____

Role 2:

_____

Role Description:_____

_____

_____

_____

_____

Role 3:

_____

Role Description:_____

_____

_____

_____

Role 4:

_____

Role Description:_____

_____

_____

_____

Role 5:

_____

Role Description:_____

_____

_____

_____

Role 6:

_____

Role Description:_____

_____

_____

_____

_____

MOMENT FOR MEDITATION

CREATE A MASTER PLAN

Here is where the magic starts. Gather all of the research, your vision, your mission statement, your avatar profile and the information of your competitors for use when developing your plan.

As you create your master plan, include benchmarks that will allow you to keep your finger on the rate of your progress. Take the major goal then break it down into bite size pieces. Set a timeline for each of your smaller targets, and then create a plan on how to reach each one.

List Your Vision:

_____

_____

_____

_____

_____

_____

_____

_____

_____

MOMENT FOR MEDITATION

It's Time To Write The Play

Break down your mission into small chunks.

Goal 1:

_____

_____

_____

How will you meet your Goal 1?

_____

_____

_____

_____

_____

What people do you need in place to complete this task?

_____

_____

_____

How much money do you need to accomplish this target? What other resources do you need to achieve success?

_____

_____

_____

_____

_____

_____

MIND MAP FOR HITTING GOAL #1

_____

_____

_____

_____

_____

_____

_____

_____

_____

_____

_____

_____

_____

It's Time To Write The Play

Break down your mission into small chunks.

Goal 2:

_____

_____

_____

How will you meet your Goal 2?

_____

_____

_____

_____

_____

_____

What people do you need in place to complete this task?

_____

_____

_____

How much money do you need to accomplish this target? What
other resources do you need to achieve success?

_____

_____

_____

_____

_____

_____

MIND MAP FOR HITTING GOAL #2

_____

_____

_____

_____

_____

_____

_____

_____

_____

_____

_____

_____

_____

_____

MOMENT FOR MEDITATION

It's Time To Write The Play

Break down your mission into small chunks.

Goal 3:

_____

_____

_____

How will you meet your Goal 3?

_____

_____

_____

_____

_____

What people do you need in place to complete this task?

_____

_____

_____

How much money do you need to accomplish this target? What
other resources do you need to achieve success?

_____

_____

_____

_____

_____

_____

MIND MAP FOR HITTING GOAL #3

_____

_____

_____

_____

_____

_____

_____

_____

_____

_____

_____

_____

_____

_____

Chapter 6
Execute

Ready. Set. Hut!

Sometimes the hardest part to fulfilling vision is starting; but once the play is in motion, it will continue until it is complete. When we are moving from the dream to the action phase, our minds often kick it into high gear and begin to over analyze or re-think all of the planning that we've done. No one wants to fail, because of how it makes us feel or how we perceive that it makes us look.

When you think about it, every successful person has at least made one failed attempt at something. Moving forward will require you to think differently about what it means when things do not work out the way that we plan. Sometimes, you are going to have to call an audible, a change in the play while your team is in motion. It is okay. You have already prepared for this.

As the leader, the weight of endeavor feels like it is squarely on your shoulders. You might be right, but that does not mean that you have to do it all alone. Your team, your community, and your organization are counting on you to pull the trigger and activate the plan that you have put so much time, energy and resources into creating.

The difference between a dreamer and a true visionary is action. You have a great plan, a winning strategy and a championship team. Show your faith in the process, your people, your vision and yourself by making the leap necessary to put your plan into action.

Make personnel changes when necessary and do not shy away from creating a new method to reach your goal, if the one you chose did not work.

What type of events, emotions or concerns could keep you from going through with your plan?

_____

_____

_____

_____

_____

_____

_____

_____

_____

Time Management Is Key.

Follow the timeline that you created and be ready for anything. There should be a time in your day for reflection, exercise, and recreation, as well as for vision inspired activities.

When you take control of your days, weeks, and months, you'll find it easier to make decisions, put meetings on the calendar and find space to do the routine tasks that may not be exciting, but are crucial to your success.

Your team members should have a timeline for completing their projects. It is your responsibility to follow up with these assigned tasks so that nothing falls through the cracks.

You don't have to micro-manage to have great follow through. Simply schedule a time on your calendar to do a progress check and find out if you need to answer any questions or help your team to get over any hurdles.

It's important that your supporters know that you are available to assist them. When you make time for success and follow through, it is much easier to deal with unexpected challenges and opportunities.

You may print out and use the planner pages at the end of the playbook to help you take control of your time

Stay Focused on the Play

Expect challenges. You cannot control every aspect of your launch, so there are bound to be some unexpected circumstances that could threaten your progress. In the event that you face a huge obstacle, do not stop.

Defeat every giant that rears its head while you are moving through your targets. These giants can be from outside sources, like current events or the economy; but sometimes the giants to your progress can be internal.

Keep your eyes open for potential leaks.

Do not allow small distractions to become major disturbances because you ignored them. Check up on your team and get consistent feedback about their insights into what's going on. Keep yourself accountable by staying in communication with your coach.

After your team reaches a goal, get ready to do it all over again to keep getting stellar results. Make necessary adjustments and give yourself permission to start again.

Rest

After every major play, you and your team will need time to rejuvenate and regroup. Make time for this important self-care act.

Rest your mind and your body. Resting gives your body, soul and spirit time to re-acquaint yourself with who you are and learn who you are becoming. This new knowledge will help you to be a better leader.

MOMENT FOR MEDITATION

REFLECTIONS

During your time of rest, write down your observations and instruct your team to do the same.

Have you changed as a leader? If your answer is yes, please explain how.

_____

_____

_____

_____

_____

_____

What have you learned about yourself?

_____

_____

_____

_____

_____

_____

What did you learn about your process?

_____

_____

_____

_____

_____

What went well during this process? What strategies will you continue to use?

_____

_____

_____

_____

_____

_____

What would you do differently the next time?

_____

_____

_____

_____

_____

_____

Remember, knowing who you are and how you operate is one of the most important components of great leadership.

Stay in the Ready Position.

READY POSITION

THIS IS THE FUNDAMENTAL POSITION FROM WHICH YOUR MUST LEAD. (BASIC TO ALL ENDEAVORS) YOU HAVE TO BE READY BEFORE YOU CAN RUN, PLAN, ACT , CHANGE, etc....

GOOD BASE- YOUR PERSONAL FOUNDATION IS SET. YOU KNOW WHO YOU ARE AND WHEREYOU ARE GOING.

GET YOUR STANCE RIGHT- BE FIRM IN YOUR PURPOSE, BUT BE READY FOR ANYTHING.

KNEES BENT – KNOW YOUR STRATEGY. BE PREPARED WITH YOUR PLAN B. THIS MUST BE DONE TO BE READY TO MOVE IN WHATEVER DIRECTION IS NECESSARY.

ARMS IN FRONT – YOU MUST BE FACING FORWARD, NOT LOOKING BEHIND YOU AT PAST MISTAKES OR BECOMING BOGGED DOWN WITH THE AFFAIRS OF THE DAY.

HEAD UP AND EYES OPEN! –REACHING YOUR GOALS REQUIRES VISION. YOU MUST BE ABLE TO SEE THE ROAD AHEAD AND RESPOND APPROPRIATELY.

BE BALANCED – USE SELF DISCIPLINE AT ALL TIMES. BE BALANCED IN HOW YOU APPROACH EACH NEW RELATIONSHIP, OPPORTUNITY AND OBSTACLE THAT ARISES.

Never allow yourself to become complacent with your success. Commit to become better with each new endeavor and you will see the world around you transform into what you dreamt it would become.

REMEMBER You Are A Power of One Leader! YOU CREATE REALITY!

Additional Resources from iCreate Inc. International

The Power of One Leadership Academy

The Power of One Leadership Academy was designed to help people and organizations discover and develop their maximum potential. With a goal to illuminate personal gifts, talents, and abilities to manifest the life skills, soft skills, and business skills needed to succeed, holistically. In a nutshell our academy cultivates winners.

While providing motivation, inspiration and opportunities to learn soft and hard skill sets and tools for leaders from around the world to progress with all they need to reach their true potential.

Power of One Bootcamps

As a coaching and business development enterprise, our hand-tailored distinct workshops are empower people from all career and business levels to reach their full potential as leaders.

We offer our Bootcamps in both live and online formats for leaders, managers and small business owners, as well as youth groups, and ministries. We have Power of One Bootcamp options for everyone.

Power of One Leadership Coaching

iCreate offers personalized Life and Leadership coaching sessions to empower leaders and organizations to meet their goals and walk with them through their process of growth and leadership.

In an ever-changing world, change never really stops and those people and organizations that don't intentionally plan for growth and evolve, eventually lose their relevance and die. That's why our team is here to prepare you for anything while we ensure you come out on top.

We'll meet on a personal level and help you set actionable steps that yield the individual and professional results you've always wanted. Let us hold you accountable for your goals while giving you the boost you need to learn, grow, and maximize your impact.

The Power of One Youth Leadership Program

iCreate Inc. International and Youth Entrepreneurs have partnered to give students with a passion for entrepreneurship a program to propel our future leaders in the world of business.

Participants can take advantage of this transformational course where they will participate in unique and interactive classes. This program is for students in schools, community centers, organizations and for churches where we customize the program to fit the groups' needs.

Every student enrolled will have the opportunity to learn about leadership, business, and other life skills necessary for starting a business and/or having a successful career field.

They will also have access to meeting and learning from real entrepreneurs with the advantage of internship and scholarship opportunities needed to set them apart in this competitive society. This is how we change lives, by giving real students, real opportunities.

If you or your organization wishes to give the youth of Atlanta access to this free course click the link to register now.

For more info or to get started visit www.icreateleadership.org

Bibliography

COLLINS ENGLISH DICTIONARY - COMPLETE & UNABRIDGED 2012
     DIGITAL EDITION. (2012). *Dictionary.com*. Retrieved from
     Dictionary.com:
     https://www.dictionary.com/browse/identity?s=ts

Jankowski, J. (2016). The ID16 Personality Types in a Nutshell. In J.
     Jankowski. Logos Media.

Murphy, J. (2010). *The Power of Your Subconscious Mind, Unlock the
     Secrets Within*. New York, New York: Penguin Group.

[1] (COLLINS ENGLISH DICTIONARY - COMPLETE & UNABRIDGED 2012 DIGITAL EDITION, 2012)

[2] (Murphy, 2010)

[3] (Jankowski, 2016)

[4] (Jankowski, 2016)

[5] (COLLINS ENGLISH DICTIONARY - COMPLETE & UNABRIDGED 2012 DIGITAL EDITION, 2012)

Made in the USA
Columbia, SC
08 June 2020

98603371R00079